Virgula by Sasja Janssen

Translated by Michele Hutchison

ADVANCE READING COPY:
PROTOTYPE POETRY

RRP: £12
ISBN: 978-1-913513-50-4
Publication date: 13 February 2024

For PR enquiries contact Rory Cook:
rory@prototypepublishing.co.uk

Contents

VIRGULA

the night I was impregnated

talk to me

there where he has a student sing

we go deeper

there is eternity in height

you leave me here with that dingy room

I love birch trees

I CALL UPON YOU

because the jackdaws are ignoring me

now I'm less able to handle the little things

as I drive a spade

because the chestnut tree in front of the prison

now I'm climbing out of the ditch

and I have risen from my first murder

because each day begins

now the little things are big

and I see them fly off again

VIRGULA

the morning is a wound

the metal under the mattress

I still need to teach the horse to swim

when the hours fall through the ceiling

my new husband has a dead wife

a drop falls into my glass of milk

there's no wind

Virgula

Virgula,

the night I was impregnated, he was a soft red,
I cried with life, but filled with emptiness I was prescribed
bedrest and my pillows are plumped every day
fluffy blankets are combed and a volley of shots blasts
storms from the sky, nothing may disturb my belly,
the only thing I am allowed to do is write letters,
or preferably sleep, half leaning against the walls hung
with green fabric and gold rings to fool the devil

I write to you because you hover in the corner of my eye
I write to you because you never answer
I write to you because, like me, you dislike stagnation

the wind begins to draw infernally from the middle of
the room, directly above my bed, the shutters creak
the curtains sway their weight, until a small tornado
rises from my lap and my belly bulges like a balloon
in the night clad with green and gold rings, the sheets are
boiled and I am visited by the midwife who sits on the high bed
with restless legs, we are shown the bible and
I laugh with life

the midwife claps her hands at my unusual
statistically-unfeasible status, the Holy Scriptures aside, calls me
a daughter of Lot and preaches to my staff
about Noah's ark but pins two pale butterflies
to the wall right through the golden eyes, as though to remind me

of my suffering, my happiness is hushed and the nights,

though clad in green with golden rings, fluoresce

and the days become jammed in a vermillion dawn

I write because I cannot utter a word

I write because the midwife has stuck her spade into me

I write because I am ashamed of my nursling

a thunderstorm-sun sneaks silver through the cracks

in the shutters, a strip of dust dances like ears of corn and every

night the midwife shovels emptiness into me, and on the eighth

morning a priest-white cloud the size of an orange

drifts into the room, directly above my bed, I blow all

my maternal love toward it but the cloud moves defiantly

back and forth before hovering midpoint, never before

have I been this alone, anxiety races through my veins

the midwife wafts the cloud to my breasts so I can

nurse it, but it results in nothing more than a nebulous nipple,

people grow restless and order us to go for a walk and

in the sun the cloud dances above my head, the way you can,

and when it rains, it leaves hailstones behind on the pavement,

sometimes I whisper cloudy words to appease it, at first I'm light-footed

but soon the walks become oppressive, as though the cloud

is conspiring with the open air outdoors

and when I'm about to snap, you stick your sting into the cloud

causing it to burst onto the fabric-clad wall, a tongue of light

is visible, a rumble of thunder, Virgula, my mind has emptied,

and again my belly swells, I can no longer see my feet,

again the midwife returns with her restless legs and her spade,
she stokes the emptiness and the bump becomes enormous, we expect
the worst, a leaden quadrangle cut from the watery-grey air,
don’t entreat me, I’m writing to you in all earnestness, Virgula Virgula.

Virgula,

talk to me about the way the flames contract and the hours expand,
the way the windows suck oxygen as they half fall onto their metal
hinges and a cool snake slides low

over the wall to the gravel border, around the reed clumps like witches' pyres
to the old woman on her fennel plot, she doesn't wave
to my twin sister, but to me with a weary hand

I am still a child, but have three lovers, a girl with ash blonde hair,
a boy for whom my knowledge of my body falls short and the teacher
who dips his Dunhill fingers into me

Virgula, the way that bed turns into rough sisal, where the night fever
in his hands and the way he tells me I must go naked to the black
wing chair with the curtains open?

in and out with corn circles on my knees, you can't do it twice
in the same bed, he says like Heraclitus, his spunk sour
as I sit wide-legged

the cherry tree looks up to the flames and a swarm of cyclists
race past the low body of the farm, they shout at
the farmer who whacks his awkward goat from the road

we smell the sharp-green green of the maize leaves
and besides the well I knit cables into a sweater for the teacher,
until the roofer steps on a nail and bellows like a bull

night-time in a quiet bath and we drink hot coffee,
our cups sway, he presses the water back into me
and I cry as he bites me into concubinage

four mornings the sissing, crunching, popping of hellish
tongues before the roof has burned off and in the night the man
fucks me again until he falls asleep on top of me with cumbersome cheeks

a smiling seahorse lies on my sister's bedside table next to some
grey atoms, she won't lend me her sleeveless sweater, I call her
a stupid baby, but she's already talking about Marx and the Sandinistas

and Jesus doesn't lumber into her bedroom, he whistles
hell under my turquoise beams and above my pine three-quarter
size bed covered with its crocheted spread there's a girl in a tutu

she has a fully-grown bedroom, its beams red as wine pulp
and her violin case rests against the tanned linen chest,
she lived more often than me and never died as I did with the man
at dusk we walk bearing torches of black plumes
we see the freshness of the elderflowers and we eat six kinds of apple
from the cellar and clear summer soup with spider

the man and I perform his lamentations, me on my tin whistle,
he on his ebony one from England, his yellow fingers
pour champagne for my return journey through the fields

no one is allowed to mention it but the white girl and

the boy come for a living room concert, my eyes smart and later
I kiss her under a heart-shaped moon that stains the darkness with ochre

and after they've gone he says he had a vision of me letting the boy
catch me with his cherubic paws, the girl who sleeps
between my legs, he makes me parade around his room, Virgula
and the next day a different girl with rabbit's teeth
and wavy black hair clings to him, surrounded by white roses,
as many as seven vases around them, I wait outside until I can drape myself across

his chic furniture one last time, I see us stretched out on a deathbed,
the girl, the boy, my twin sister, only the man
breaths between us, Virgula

he covers me in his dressing gown with the birds and instructs me
on the Final Things, his smoke like a morning breeze
over my face and he whispers obligatory hate is love love is nothing

Virgula, what do you do when the fires blaze and the hours shrink,
how do you escape in your memories, how do you die
without dreams, how do you die alone if you were born together?

Virgula,

there where he has a student sing, his right hand waving
aristocratically as he summons someone next to the stage
proceeds to smoke himself blue,
mummy's boy who can't get away from this stinking peatbog, bawls
his lungs out on the stage, I practise my laughing skills there,
there where it smells of burnt dust and hot and cold draughts
brush past you like underwater, the little iron stove
near the window singes your legs, you wear men's shoes and your
hair smells of manure and needs combing, the boy who
fancies me whispers, he strokes my knee under our school desk,
where no one knows the word lechery,
we think about death, but I'm already being praised, I'm being praised
that's where the foreplay begins

and in our free period we drink bitter coffee with Cointreau,
there in his bare flat he lives in a book, because black hair
blue eyes, he points to himself as if I didn't know that one
but I'm no actress and I live with a girl's cunt, in the rooms
without curtains where he opens me upon a sisal rug
and why isn't there any sex in your stories, Virgula,
and later it rains and we walk across the peat, my skirt drags
through the mud and I think about the girls who aren't allowed
to go to his class, but my skirt is already bathing in the upstairs bath,
everything revolves around you

suicide is painless, watch out he sways giddily to the music,
only for you, my jaw is hurting,

everything revolves madly around you,

as though I didn't know that, but I fill my mouth with his salty cock

and count back down from a hundred, and in the chilly bath

he chucked me out of, I let out a high-pitched laugh

to cherish what I can still do in abandonment,

I'm in a hurry, a hurry to make my mind

fly upwards to the golden butterflies.

Virgula,

we go deeper, past the Indian Ocean in which the island bathes
my bare girlish legs burn on the hot engine, my hair is made
of gold, we don't wear helmets because terrorists wear those
but you have morphine in a felt bag around your neck, in case we end up
flailing on the roadside, in case the food poisons us,
later when you get a yellow suit made and buy a sitar
from a brahman,
Virgula, I can no longer picture it

his sinewy penis, the way he clenched his teeth when he wrote,
his skinny ribcage

in the evening the curfew hour and the inky blackness quivers and
we fuck on a mattress with faded sunflowers
until we can fuck no more,
you're a nymphomaniac you say
but I'm nauseous and feel a presence behind my back,
it's a tarantula that won't be chased away,
maybe it smells the sunflowers, maybe it smells our sex,
you sweep it up and shake it out of a towel into the night garden
but the next day it's back

we line our eyes with kohl and wear our clothes a cool
silken yellow

during the daytime I feed orphans rice with milk and cardamom, they slap
the table with their palms and scream in their cots

when a snake slips inside, the other carers shriek
chase away the snake with cloths, they're just as young as me and
clap their hands briefly because I don't understand them,
then the sky turns a darkened ochre,
different kinds of rain fall at the same time

the island was suicidal, not I, not there in the tropics,
not with you

we dig wells in villages and drive for days on the black
city motorbike that hangs low on the bends, over crossroads
where goats and dogs lie down, they look at us like people,
large and astonished,
and women lift up their crying babies
to be taken, we leave them behind and the air smells of oil
and my eyes water soot

you martyr of my forgetting

you accidentally buy a hundred condoms that the chemist counts out
for us on the counter, he bares his dirty teeth in embarrassment
and points at me, I've been saving it for this country,
the country is horny, not I, I say in Dutch,
it's because of the divi divi trees, the palms, the snakes, the hot wind
I saved it for him, his skinny body
the reason they call him Biafra here

you serve up only loose ends now, no soil, skin, voice, smell, time

tomorrow when you've gone to Jaffna for a war council
I'll eat rambutan, I'll boil tea on the stove consecrated with milk
and I'll lie in the gloom on the blood-red floor,
at night I'll curl up against the wall afraid of the spider,
I'll picture you being shot dead
but when you're back we drive to Galle, where beans
are still called boontjes, we don't talk about the colonial
past, the horror is where the kookaburras laugh and laugh

we wore our lust lightly

in the early evening you drink beer with men in a pub
I'm not allowed to enter and a man masturbates on a bridge
because my hair is made of gold and the night falls abruptly,
we wipe the kohl from our eyes and sleep in damp cloths
on mattresses with bed bugs but it isn't long
before I'm pregnant with a little boy
whom I'll never see again, just like you

we go deeper.

Virgula,

there is eternity in height, there is eternity
in hanging from a height
longing sometimes to remove the distance between sky and earth,
to let yourself drop just past the short gardens with empty benches fridges
plants bicycles, but mostly there's a longing
to enter the sky like a room

my room that consists of a large window and has no
centre, there is some cheating with a square,
in it a low bed, cheese cloth used as curtain, pale blue
linoleum like a clear February
a small table suitable for a single chair, when you wash
the window from the outside the depth spins beyond your shoulder

Virgula, you were here too, in the closeness you can touch
the four small walls, the concrete with knots of air that rot
in the stairs stuck to the side of the building,
my eyes live with the greyish-yellow concrete from which rectangular
rooms have been carved for students, sometimes I imagine them as dogs
maybe because they fuck in the afternoon

there is the eternity of calm window, planes disappear into it
when I lie on my low bed
which isn't mine but belongs to the flat and
I think of the girl down the corridor in her smart apartment,
always dressed in a twinset, the Afghan who cooks bones in oil,
the young Iranian who shows me drawings, his eyelashes are butterflies

it's like they don't exist when I'm in my room
having to read P.C. Hooft until a boy
with murky eyes kisses me in the room next to my own,
he has nothing left, he says, except for a raised bed a fridge
a stereo, we take a young cat from the pet shop that falls from the snowy
balcony rails three weeks in, the days are as still as winter

I celebrate Christmas with the boy in an almost empty tower block
I count how many rooms on the other side have their curtains
shut, we laze around and cook our chickens,
nuts, no plums, we watch *Der blaue Engel*
on the flat's tv channel and smoke rollies
the stringy tobacco tastes of smoked blood

in the new year we get two more cats, the white one is mine
the black-and-white one his,
until I move to a different block of flats because we've broken up,
we split the metal cutlery
the bleach I used to scrub the bathroom so I can hand back
the place clean make me and the cats throw up

and that's where you really come to life, Virgula,
in the view of a large spruce tree, in the green solitude,
I spend one last night with the boy, then the morning
blares for me to leave and I steal the low bed
with my woolly blanket, stiff with age, the white cat
and together we wait, we wait for someone to fetch us from this room

I hang rattan in front of the window you rattle at, I get a sideboard from the street and paint it white,

it's no use, all of eternity has moved house with me, Virgula.

Virgula,

you leave me here with that dingy room like a snow globe in my hand
the room damp and in the middle the bed wide-legged
on rugs on acrid yellow wooden floors, not ochre,
nothing with a c is given the chance to sicken under the crown
spread above them

there is a boy, a girl with her March fruit,
they laugh each other's breath away, dampness stings, lust seizes and you
press me against the window steamed up from the stove,
a rock-hard tulip on the mantelpiece, a three of hearts in the edge of the mirror,
a cat in a crib, I close my eyes

he comes from a city that insults the sea, the dunes black
on the water, clouds of smoke on the waves, but here in the backyard
chickens pluck at the idyll invented by his ancestors,
there is a boy, a girl for you from softer soil where God
not dead because you still can

where apple trees crooked and plums hang, she must come with me
to the old country and drowns beneath a moon's
halo because you can, he feeds her razor clams like fingers
from the pan, the liver sandy on the tongue, his language is coarse
but he pisses like a girl, and that land teems with earthy smells

and every morning my darkness expires and you shake the room out
from under my bed, rugs billow, lamps swing,
the cat flies up in all that yellow, and her motionless in a cross

on top of each other, arms spread, legs flat, no breath
around them that is alive, Virgula!

you give me more than snow in a globe, their sheets between
the trees before the seawall, underwear on the hedge, a jay in the net
over the cherries recipient of his bullet, medlars that the boy parts in two
like her vulva, thousands of berries turn their tongues red
what do I have to do with them, tell me that, what do they do to me

until I bear the child, behold a son with their free name
until I bear the child, on a stool in front of a blossoming stove,
but it doesn't take long, a few fast shakes
and I lose all three of them to your fire stoking my homesickness
when I see one last sparrow darting from the sparks, Virgula.

Virgula,

I love birch trees
in their fragile haziness
and one ungainly afternoon it gets too much
loving those scorched white things that are accused of all sorts
women of the forest
spearheads of melancholy
belly milk good for a thousandfold strength
birch wine for your mood
grammar of light and always willing
to receive any kind of wisdom
their almost human embrace
but seldom seen for what they really are

I hear they lost their spirit
to their own roots
their skin to roofs bags baskets
their innards to glue and the hairless,
before you know it they are infringing on the tree line
like their pitiful fellows
so I take my house under my arm
torn loose like the page of a substantial book,
I'm a poor reader of other people's lies
but a few miles further where snow-powdered cathedrals
bore into skies of lead and glass
where each day is a midsummer's midnight, let alone a midday,
I empty the household effects over the sea
my theremin is all I need

beneath the disastrous trees the local population

the women sing the praises of saws, their ugly teeth

soft, thin, bloody to quieten anything,

I switch saw lines and snigger at my trophy

the children bite me like cats

the woodchoppers down a schnapps on my veranda

and soon I receive instruction on writing poetry (already can)

forging metal (everything comes down to form) and soothsaying

(nothing more poetic than the truth)

she skips the lessons in medicine when she sees

my emerald inlaid pillboxes,

I am your preacher of all preachers

and my smile is generous and forgiving

and with a wanton right hand and a refined left hand

I begin my vaudeville

undulating sirens soften the coppery sky

flowing into the roots and then out again,

my veil caresses all the crowns, of people and leaves

the trees blow free their white dresses,

never before have my hands sung such a consolation song

fiery midsummer hours' long,

my right hand ever closer my left ever closer

the children they howl like wolves

the men drowning their bitterness

the birches proud of their twig hairdos,

people are sleeping soundly again, people are giving birth to new days,

until an unmistakable silence descends

wife of the devil

trader of false notes, your grammar obscure

your veil synthetic, the green unnatural,

I will let you hunt me down that final afternoon,

the woodcutters cleave my theremin, its antennae

bound to branches like strange fruit

I am nowhere without, not in this forest

my splintered house, not in my true mind

rather exaggerated, this anger,

people prise the trees open again, guzzle their milk wine water

everything snaps and kissed the ground

the entire forest chopped down for personal gain,

crazy for people who swear by their own tree bubble

so I take my truth under my arm

and leave the trees forever

there is always one person who doesn't believe me

or love me

but there isn't anyone who repeats my words

no one with the same awkward spirit

no one who can light up a whole forest

and this electrifies my brief happiness, before I disappear

behind the cathedrals.

I call upon you

I call upon you,

because the jackdaws are ignoring me on a branch at a distance

they never land on my balcony, they don't beady-eye my presence

for a single moment, nor the traveller in front of the prison

three trees' widths away, his leather bags gathered around his feet

like dogs, yawning slack-tongued at a country that once

dangled in the arms of a river, he doesn't see me either, back

I go to the house of my birth.

I call upon you,

now I'm less able to handle the little things and that one incident
kicked the other along like tumbleweed, not without danger
like the time I veered off the road and relieved myself in a ditch next to the Aa's
feeble stream behind me a bull that wanted to
slaughter its own meadow, not without danger
like when they cut off my breast to get close to my
heart and all I could hear was the lowing of cattle.

I call upon you,

as I drive a spade through the neck of a wounded blackbird,
its parents dance an arm's length away from me,
and the way I bury it warm in a crock where the heat
makes the white of the walls, the white doors, the white roof shine
in the scent of burned lavender, only a bird murderer
knows how to use spectacle to unburden yourself of yourself before returning
to the city where I proceed to call out for you, for the third time.

I call upon you,

because the chestnut tree in front of the prison weighs its white plumes
in late flamingo light, it raises its arms when I shelter under its
dome, an abandoned dog foams around the trunk and eats
an apple from my hand, until black slides across the pink
and the horse-branches stop swishing and see how the moon
is leering at me like a big eye, with slight scratches on its eyeball
drawn by a pen with a steady hand.

I call upon you,

now I'm climbing out of the ditch maybe just a dozen royal rods
wide, I see how naked the hazel tree is screaming, I scream you
back, and in an empty barn a desiccated cat clings to the beams,
I fling open the table doors for the traveller
he's come a long way, just like me, sitting with a candle and a pen at a horse-brown
table drawing your face on a nerved leaf, my heart is bald
and can no longer write to you.

I call upon you,

and I have risen from my first murder, it scares
the birds away, not without danger, like when I beat life into the cat
and allowed the table doors to conspire with the wind, not without danger,
like when I climbed the chestnut tree to wait for the other jackdaws like
a jackdaw, I tell them from my seething-hot balcony,
the birds laugh me out of my desolation
but at last I am seen.

I call upon you,

because each day begins with a portrait of you, a wave to the wind
except for the hours when our thatched roof was burned
to crackling dust, not far from the river Aa and on a side road
in the village pub I find a couple praying like mad,
I don't know what for, under their table their cardboard suitcases
just like mine, still, it's not you they look to, they call upon a different deity
and they'll leave this village, just like me.

I call upon you,

now that the little things are big and I can bear some seriousness, I don't want to
be anywhere anymore, the barn with table doors a stab wound in the countryside
the sun too hot, the wind too much, the hazel tree hangs heavy and
the painterly clouds chase me, so I jump out of the ditch
and I walk the breadth of hundreds of trees back and chase the traveller
away from the prison, spiders crawl from his eyes
his dogs begin to bark.

I call upon you,

and I see them fly off again, the jackdaws, they plunge into the shared garden
they don't beady-eye me, I eat my displacement from
my own palm and a large leaf unfolds from my heart
for you, I no longer care who slaughters the grass,
marks the sky, which eye sees me, and my voice becomes lighter
until the only thing left is whether you understand me and
will find my empty breast.

Virgula

Virgula,

the morning is a wound that only becomes animated when you arrive
here still twilight, drizzly mist, though night broke free of its hinges
and me from my white suit with stars like ash,
so that thing with its back to you on the bed is my body, who would
touch it these days?

the morning hovers where you hover
in this same half-light, half-hearted potato darkness, dewy sadness
now I awaken beneath the portrait of Nusch, compact flower
no dung fly can open her eyes, my flutter-fingers,
I come from a wedding I wasn't invited to

a blue ribbon adorns her head rendering her female with half body
boy's breasts with nipples like shot-out eyes, those donkey's ears of clay
not hers, the neck too tight for the mystery of the world, Virgula!
too many chairs around my bed, they puff out their cushions
due to a lack of guests, all things stiff grey back in their shape
except for me

out of hundreds I bought her
for just one euro, Amfortas, save me from that skinny neck
from this neck with goods and chattels, crockery with finger grease, assaulted paper
covered in slashes, you dip your sting in, try out your goading there, Virgula
with your mediaeval blockhead always singing the same tune

visions of a loss against the walls my cliffs
the darkness dilutes still further, flaxy light weaves disquiet, I don't cry out day

to the curtains, the wardrobe with lungs, the ceiling with eyes, the chairs
the bloody chairs, a corsage on a pin flaps next to my bed, go by
maybe I was screwed last night
and outside the August moon shimmers, then you join us

without sound, shards as the sublime breaks
the windows whole and ajar, the door shut high
like hours ago my shirt, the suit a snakeskin on the floor
maybe I was castrated last night but no one beside me
on the springs, so that there on the bed is my corpse, who tidies
those up nowadays?

the morning falls with stardust into my mouth
the snake on my bone but I cannot get up and I see
you on every chair like a family member praying for an easier life,
the light from entertainment that animates me, the way you turned the corners
of the room inside out, how do I bring this madness
to an end?

you unlace my Nusch, my flower
and she says I overplayed my hand, I understand, I gambled her away
and she laughs shrilly from my wall, yes, the eyes
in the ceiling, the walls icily clean
the chairs stacked, but I loved her so, we didn't last a day,
we didn't last a night, don't bury me in the afternoon, she-devil,

Virgula.

To accompany Picasso's portrait of Nusch Eluard, *Madame Paul Eluard*, 1941

Virgula,

the metal under the mattress bounces as you dart before my eyes
quivering dragonfly of glass
and me who has to report to the guardian of my archives

a stack of pink-dotted files, a kind of baby between us
but she keeps quiet, she keeps a low profile on the dirty Formica,
I'm the crying animal here

the morning pointy with luminosity, trees with their bones
in the sparse green, roadsides with gnawing hunger
people drowned in one another and the stones alive and without me

the canal made of oil colours and I cycle to the tower
of the implementing body, where a red line sews the rooms
a Ficus pushed into the corner, I stroke its fabric

my gospel is voluminous, the baby
and somewhere in a basement corridor dossiers of a more forgotten nature
my carnal secrets and things that never end

there on the Formica my bulging navel too now
the guardian pinches it and nobody knows what else to do with you
in our light that betrays no course of action

glassmakers, martyrs, I know the poltergeists in your mind
and in the morning a Virgula torments you, your cat lays eggs
you can't fool me, but my watery-grey gaze

dreams him to his mother, she hangs up the washing and always
that blowing of sheets on a wire
he no longer has to fix me on a spring roof made of asphalt

while back home a new wife awaits him in his Auping
a Pole to whitewash all the walls around
the moles in his circular garden, they will be gassed tonight

I fear his cruel summation
the implantation laws in which I collapse
I fear the limitations he cuts my thoughts with

the human being dissipates, I told him, look through the windows that
never open, but he wants my thumb
with the sickness of all sicknesses in a diabolical form

until the baby screams her legs rigid in that purposeful carpeted room
like a scorched field of potatoes,
the line to the outside is short and roundabout in roundabout

I cry to the birds, they wave back with the ease of their world
and at home I unlock all the doors and windows, I call everyone, they only answer
I write them all letters and immediately receive the right answer, yes

bless my comma, things aren't that bad
I get another year to subjugate the animal, then I bounce up
to you and at last the morning comes behind my back and

finally the morning comes into itself.

Virgula,

I still need to teach the horse to swim

but seasick from my amble I lie on the flagstones
in the hall, no river or lake to hand except for an unhewn
canal with broken pounders along the side, patchy suns
on their hand palms now the evening is aflame, I have so much to do,
done nothing wrong nothing good, only cooperated,
hurry up before the water goes out

the incandescent geese screech back at the Kostverlorenkade
ban the centaur from my door, its shadowy lurk
appeal to the moon, the moon like a bar of soap under water
for some light and my offspring,
his cries too high-pitched for his mother to hear, he lies there
like a leper with spindly limbs, his tong draws breath from the ice
don't leave him there next to the raging deep-freeze
not a single flapping game left in this house, no writing you
I no longer like you

and the evening primrose is dying yellow again

and everything cracks with dryness as though it is raining
it cracks with wrath, enough evil for the calyxes
to be nipped in the bud, enough late evenings
for the bees, they come with its sugary death,
can't even be counted, all those openings,
they spirit away my eyes

but just as well their repeated floral death
they could kill a mule, my horse, with their crowns
and imprison me in their yellow limbo, flat on the slabs
mirror that only mirrors itself like a frozen pond

in this night-nightly light
which I saved up for, the door wide wide
for deeper air and the hall that encloses me, enough nights
that we go under, the flower and me and the horse
already flowing from its form, its cow-eyes from horse's sockets
his plait releases my hair, not chestnut or plaited all in white
but razed by the centaur who has
the oldest equine pain who has the longest-held rights
to the flagstones that hold me down

so blood hot that it crackles with aridity as though it has snowed

and the moon saponifies the canal, the geese smack into the hall
the offspring outplays himself, hear his limbs flapping
his leprous lightness moth-like,
I must not forget him, I must put the light with the heavy
but overnight the night has become blacker ice,
I step away from the floor, then I unriddle the water with tender
irises for the horse, its bullrushes
hide the lust of his beating hooves, his broad stable breath
but I ruffle my sweetness

he comes, Virgula, you don't even come that hard, my entangled,
what did I do wrong that my pelvis keeps rotting

what should I do about darkening, about writing to you,
I believe that my soul is two mules
but just as well, the mules, they drown a belief
that doesn't exist, the horse solidifies in my bloody pelvis

and I hide in the chest cavity of the night like a nomad
inside a camel

and I laugh a short-hard laugh

and I kill

and a blazing punch kills the entire darkness.

Virgula,

when the hours fall through the ceiling in the late front room
with a view over the courtyard with its hundreds of knee-high plants
and flat orchids, they rattle me

when the hours fall through the ceiling and you take cover under my desk
and the mirror expires in shards on my wooden floor

when the hours fall through the ceiling, I leave you behind, move through the hounded
grasses and my breast spied in an oil-shined pond

she floats next to a lily named Victoria that sometimes blooms white
and smells of pineapple, I catch my breast with a butterfly net
like the lily a small child with her leaf, that sometimes blooms pink

surrounded by trees with writerly names like the handkerchief tree,
bitternut hickory, date-plum, but now I have regret on my hands
where it shrivels from stingray to sweetbread

is that the cancer I ask her, but my heart stings and the next night I make
the hours kneel but my breast is gone, perhaps returned to the scene of the crime

the way you always do with me, where the night smells of apple vinegar
where they keep the curtains open in front of a building with a flickering eye
on its roof, where an eviscerated woman screams

and on the toilet a man clutches his head, wails for an angel.
and I am closed in by a curtain as though I have to take a bed bath

but the nurses wheel in a mirror for me

in which I never see my breast again and in the night I limp to the pond
and glide into it but I keep finding my body on that toilet with angel's hair

until I have told Victoria a few more times about her victories and defeats,
the plants observe me from their lowly position, until I see the lily unfolding a child

and again nothing said that can't be said without a breast
in a bygone front room without light, oh Virgula.

Virgula,

my new husband has a dead wife, a body of copper and I
have a boulder in my head, it presses against my eyes, which stick out
as though I cannot see enough, but I want to stop thinking because
my husband already has a dead wife, a body of copper
a history wider than my sleep ceiling with knots
that quiver like atoms, Virgula, the boulder presses against my imminent
thoughts which constrict

in the night under the knots I see a long procession of seers
go by, mainly women with chunky jewellery
and thin lips that talk a lot, also the odd stonecutter
who refuses to cut and draws diagnoses like cards from a deck,
stop that crying, yes, I stop crying and wipe my dewy cheeks
but a boulder needs water like in a river, better to think
of your husband

and his three children, they love maths, that's why
they don't need to leave their cramped bedrooms, they drink vodka
in the linen closet and spend the whole day calling on loudspeaker, sometimes
they cycle at night along the empty Amstel in lonely clothes, death has
never existed here, but I have a son, he knows the names and uses
of different varieties of apples, pears berries plums figs nuts, he thinks
of the ending like of the beginning

and he can stay underwater for a long time with his butterfly lungs, but the boulder
folds my memories together, he rolls behind my eyes, Virgula,
you know how much crying fits in my rooms, my husband doesn't

he has a copper wife, she sits on the edge of my bed

when I cry and smile, not the seers, not the children, not my son,

it expands and expands and is as ethereal as light and I am inconsolable, is the boulder

the reason I mortally injure my thoughts?

Virgula,

a drop falls into my glass of milk and makes a crown

a circle is an expansion on its way to a square

commas sway their way to a full stop, but mine never sway

to their end

they attack me from a line of sunlight between the curtains

jostling with amusement when they latch on

the shapes are already there, but you need to find the language

to capture them in,

I long for a full stop, but my Virgulas are wary

of employing them,

I press them close as though death were breathing down my neck

as though I no longer know how to count my blessings,

and I like to count, the number 6 I love, and that is the sum of

the consecutive numbers 1, 2 and 3, the 2 is red, the 3 blue,

the 1 is probably colourless

there's a lot to say for the number thousand

the sun is mortal,

Halley's comet freed itself from a cloud of millions of comets

and seldom stops at the sun, which shortens its life, it hurries along the top

edge of our heavens every 76 years, like in the Bayeux tapestry, which is

why I won't die until 2061,

think of that, Virgula,

my thoughts form chains

the way my husband drops onto the stone floor when I leave him

the back garden in which bats fall like stars, the way he
cuts slugs in half with his Laguiole knife so that they don't leave
silvery trails on the rough carpet beneath the alcove in the wall
we bathe our child in the deep porcelain sink
that has cracked, I need to let him enjoy the water
he enjoys the water
the way his first hands are bloodied and claw at me
at our beginning we were as dark as Jesus
Halley's comet announces its own death, just like Jesus
an embroidered crowd points upwards in mortal terror
my vanished family points too, we are our own portent,
homesickness is as greedy as lust
you can fuck lust

I ponder on another head, my thoughts too great an emotion

you cry about a physicist who finds a jewel-shaped proof
for a truth we can touch but not see
the jewel on my slender ring finger
I dream up an insect-green stone for it
what on earth do you know about the contemporary, the great,
the inevitable, the spherical, the whole?
the way my husband falls again, his crossbar bike bounces from the pavement
like a ball, he catches the Gazelle in one hand and sets it straight
like a reluctant child,
language makes you lonely, Virgula!

I cannot live in my poems, it's windy, there's a threat of hurricanes
the silence strikes the earth like a square, poppies on an embankment

tumbleweed everywhere,

I don't want a break, no tumbling, I want to reach the end

in a single sweep, I want the means to break the chain

but I allow myself to be chased along

by the commas, my she-devils

I set the glass of milk that remains mottled on my desk.

Virgula,

there's no wind, fear is blowing with cadmium skies and purple
trees, but it hasn't been windy for a long time,
it is raining time, first at three o'clock in the afternoon, then at five
in the morning, times that cannot be an origin
they keep you silenced
but it's stopped raining

I pass the houses on the canal side and see the everyday everywhere
a succulent with dusty navel, tea towels on a windowsill,
a door open to a kitchen too shiny to cook in
behind it a polished garden with a nun with dark blue legs
she is smoking a cigarette on a metal
chair, her head raised to a bluer God

there is no season, roots push up stones, shadows
mottling pavements, further along opened curtains like strips of cloth
dead flies against a painted wall, a toddler in a narrow hallway
with a large pink canvas, a bathroom on the ground floor, I see
a bidet, and fish eyes on the canal as though the water is boiling
but there is no season

and on the other side a cemetery with fresh graves and insects
they are singing dies irae, there is light, there is dark and the temperature is the same
as my own, the silence strokes your forehead, I walk past the nun
at the window, she's holding an orange, stiff-lipped she says
I won't make you martyr's food
the kitchen doesn't tolerate guests

then I see you sitting there, Virgula, you curl on her folded shoulder,
you jump onto the orange, I want you back, I want you back
into my room where you belong, and then the trees bow before the graves
all the oxygen is sucked out of the everyday
the windows grow dark, I run out of the frame
from the canal to my house

where the man in his white suit with stars like ashes sits at the round table
Nusch next to him with boyish breasts and her eyes half-lidded
I see a smile that isn't painted
a boy and a girl with a snowball who have crawled out
of my poems, where are you, Virgula,
to drop them back in again?

It was good, they say, it was summer, the shadows cast shadows
the roots freshly carried by the rocks, the toddler plays with a stick
on the pavement, your bare feet in the water that was calm, calm
and a rose spiralled around the nun's legs and Virgula kept
us together, but we have been abandoned
and don't keep quiet

it was good, they say, they touch me, pinch me and
I become afraid of my own creations, you don't have to write
us together they scream as though they are singing, let us go
and there you flutter back
and land on my head like a sparrow so that I tumble into the everyday
at which point the wind rises again.

Sasja Janssen is a poet and novelist based in Amsterdam. Her first publications were two novels but since her father's death she has written mainly poetry. Her poems feature the body in many shapes, from tool to target, from weapon to wound. *Virgula* (2021) was nominated for five Dutch prizes and awarded the prestigious Awater Poetry Prize. *Putting On My Species* (2014) was her first collection to be translated into English and was published by Shearsman in 2020.

Janssen has performed nationally and internationally, including at festivals in Nicaragua, Medellín, Mexico and Buenos Aires.

The poet and critic Piet Gerbrandy wrote of her work, 'The poet tries desperately to grasp something of the insane world we find ourselves in and in which we have to simply make do, with totally inadequate means.'

Michele Hutchison was born in the UK and has lived in Amsterdam since 2004. She was educated at UEA, Cambridge, and Lyon universities. She translates literary fiction and nonfiction, poetry, graphic novels, and children's books. She also co-authored the successful parenting book *The Happiest Kids in the World*.

Virgula by Sasja Janssen, published by Prototype in 2024

Originally published as *Virgula* by Querido, Amsterdam, in 2021

A CIP record for this book is available from the British Library.

Design by Zigmunds Lapsa
Typeset in xxxxxx
Printed in xxx by xxx

ISBN 978-1-913513-50-4

The publisher gratefully acknowledges the support of the Dutch Foundation for Literature

(type 1 – poetry)
www.prototypepublishing.co.uk
@prototypepubs

prototype publishing
71 oriel road
london e9 5sg
uk

Nederlands letterenfonds
dutch foundation for literature

( ) ( ) p prototype

( ) (   )   p   prototype

poetry / prose / interdisciplinary projects / anthologies

Creating new possibilities in the publishing of fiction and poetry through a flexible, interdisciplinary approach and the production of unique and beautiful books.

Prototype is an independent publisher working across genres and disciplines, committed to discovering and sharing work that exists outside the mainstream.

Each publication is unique in its form and presentation, and the aesthetic of each object is considered critical to its production.

Prototype strives to increase audiences for experimental writing, as the home for writers and artists whose work requires a creative vision not offered by mainstream literary publishers.

In its current, evolving form, Prototype consists of 4 strands of publications:
(type 1 — poetry)
(type 2 — prose)
(type 3 — interdisciplinary projects)
(type 4 — anthologies) including an annual anthology of new work, *PROTOTYPE*.